Animals in the Wild

Giraffe

by Mary Hoffman

Raintree Publishers
Milwaukee

The giraffe is the tallest animal in the world. An adult male may measure almost eighteen feet high! Even newborn giraffes are almost six feet tall. The baby giraffe in this picture is just a few days old.

Giraffes usually have only one baby at a
time. The young giraffes have to be
protected from lions and leopards. So two
or more adult females look after the
babies in a kind of nursery while their
mothers are eating. 3

Giraffes have different skin patterns and colors. This common Masai giraffe has blotchy skin markings. Its coloring blends in with the shade of trees. This helps protect the giraffe by making it hard to see.

This reticulated giraffe has a skin pattern that looks like a fish net. Its skin patches are larger and more regular than the Masai giraffe's. This giraffe lives in Kenya. In fact, all giraffes that roam wild live in Africa.

Both male and female giraffes have short
horns covered with skin and hair. They grow
between the giraffe's ears. A second pair
sometimes grows behind the first pair.

8

The giraffe has a very long tongue. It stretches almost a foot and a half long! The tongue is very rough. It is useful in gathering twigs and leaves from treetops.

9

Leaves and flowers from the acacia tree
are the giraffe's favorite food. It wraps its
long tongue around the shoots and softens
them with saliva so it can chew them. The
tree's many thorns don't hurt the giraffe's
rough tongue.

The giraffe's neck may measure six feet or longer! But it has only seven neck bones— the same number that people have. With such long necks, male giraffes can eat leaves from the tops of trees. Females bend their necks and feed lower down.

Because of their long necks and legs, it is hard for giraffes to reach down to drink water. They must spread their front legs far apart and bend them. One giraffe keeps watch for danger while the others drink.

Giraffes usually sleep standing up. When they do lie down, they take only short naps because they could be easily attacked by lions. While lying down, a giraffe holds up its long neck or rests it on a hip.

Giraffes live together for safety in groups called herds. When danger is spotted, all the giraffes in a herd run at once. They can go quite fast—about thirty miles an hour.

Not many other animals can reach the
tops of trees, so giraffes have plenty of
food. The giraffes in this picture live
near Mount Kilimanjaro in Kenya.

The okapi is the giraffe's only relative. It lives in the rain forests of Africa. This shy animal lives by itself, not in herds. It wasn't discovered until 1900.

Giraffes are quiet, peaceful animals. But young males sometimes practice fighting by "necking." They wrap their long necks around each other and push. But they rarely hurt one another.

Giraffes live together peacefully with other animals, like the gnus in this picture. Gnus are a kind of African antelope. Many giraffes and gnus live together on the large Masai Mara Game Reserve in Kenya.

Giraffes and zebras often live together in the wild and also in zoos and wildlife parks. Except for lions and leopards, the giraffe's only enemies are people. Some giraffes are now protected from hunters.

First published in this edition in the United States of America 1986
by Raintree Publishers, 310 West Wisconsin Avenue,
Milwaukee, Wisconsin 53203.

Reprinted in 1989

First published in the United Kingdom under the title
Animals in the Wild—Giraffe
by Belitha Press Ltd.
31 Newington Green, London N16 9PU
in association with Methuen Children's Books Ltd.

Library of Congress Number: 86-6770

Dedicated to Nicholas and Emily

Scientific Adviser: Dr. Gwynne Vevers. Picture Researcher: Stella Martin.
Designer: Ken Hatherley.

Acknowledgments are due to the following for the photographs used
in this book: Bruce Coleman Ltd pp. 2, 6, 9, 11, 12/13, 14, 15, 16/17,
18 and 21; Eric and David Hosking p. 8; Frank Lane Picture Agency Ltd
pp. 4/5 and 10; Natural Science Photos pp. 7 and 19; NHPA pp. 1 and
20; Oxford Scientific Films p. 3; Survival Anglia pp. 22/23. Front and
back covers: Bruce Coleman Ltd.

ISBN 0-8172-2397-5

Library of Congress Cataloging in Publication Data

Hoffman, Mary, 1945—
   Giraffe.

(Animals in the wild)
Summary: Discusses the behavior patterns of giraffes and shows
them in their natural surroundings.
   1. Giraffes—Juvenile literature (1. Giraffes)
I. Title.   II. Series.
QL737.U56H64   1986   599.73'57   86-6770
ISBN 0-8172-2397-5 (lib. bdg.)

3 4 5 6 7 8 9 10 11 12 13   99 98 97 96 95 94 93 92 91 89